SUNBIRD

Other Books by Arthur Dobrin

A HISTORY OF BLACK JEWS IN AMERICA (1965)

THE ROLE OF AGRARIAN COOPERATIVES
IN THE DEVELOPMENT OF KENYA (1970)

GETTING MARRIED THE WAY YOU WANT (1974)

SUNBIRD

By Arthur Dobrin

Illustrated by Lyn Dobrin

Cross-Cultural Communications
Merrick, New York
1976

Copyright © 1976 by Arthur Dobrin
All Rights Reserved

Acknowledgment is made, with thanks, to the editors of the following magazines in which these poems first appeared:

Bitterroot: "An African I Met," "The Butcher Shop," "A Chorus Moving," "He Held My Hand," "Nyansarara's Circumcision," "Old People," "Trepanning."

Chelsea: "Abuya's Laugh," "At the Migori River," "Circumcision Song," "Ex-Chief Musa (1)," "Interrupted Hike," "I Snapped Her Picture," "Song of Praise," "Suicide."

Compass: "Itinerant Witchdoctor," "Twilight," "Two Nights in Uganda."

Cosmopolitan Contact: "For Nyakundi—Our Son (1)."

Dark Waters: "Kisii Market."

Ocarina (India): "Birds," "The Martyr."

Okike (Nigeria): "Kisii Warriors."

Poet (India): "Gift Giving," "A Morning in Kisii," "Our American-Born Girl," "The President Visits."

Published by
Cross-Cultural Communications
239 Wynsum Avenue, Merrick, N.Y. 11566

ISBN 0-89304-012-6 Softbound
ISBN 0-89304-013-4 Hardbound
Library of Congress Catalog Card Number: 76-53661

Designed by Bebe Barkan
Printed in the United States of America

CONTENTS

for Lyn Moraa, sunset eyes

HERE ON THE EQUATOR

Here on the equator
When the sun goes down
Night is the master.
No one fools the night
Like people who ride trains
Underground in my native city.
No fake suns try to light the sky.
The night commands respect
Without asking.
Death is closer by.
I feel the changes of the earth
And death has no fearful mask.
It is like the smell of eucalyptus,
The buzz of mosquitoes,
The flight of butterflies.
It is,
And I almost hold its hand.

A MORNING IN KISII

Vultures fly high
Over flame trees
A hundred suns of orange and yellow blooms
While the lean Zebu cow lows
Her final call.
The butcher whets his killing knife.
Mill wheels, grinding coffee cherries,
Spit pulp into the silver stream
Glimmering.
Brown beans dry,
Spread thin by kerchiefed women,
Men with rubber boots.
Mama Uji sells her gruel in
Half calabash cups,
"Senti tatu! Senti tatu!"
Spearless warriors known as cattle thieves
Wait for the magistrate.
Morning comes—
Kisii is awake.

Senti tatu—Swahili for "three cents."

KISII MARKET

A black messiah
Shouts his prayers through his beard
And preaches in a paper bullhorn,
His burning robe flowers in the sun.
A butcher covered with blood
Leaves his shop to listen.
A silent woman who has onions for hair
Fingers her money beneath her dress.
Children watch the messiah
See his lizard tongue
His eyes like dung beetles
His nails like rotting strawberries.
A snake wraps around a charmer's arm.
Whores with naked thighs
Hold smiles in their hands.
The messiah tosses Christ on the road
To busses that belch
And scavengers that swoop by the stream.
The messiah hurls his words through his beard
In a language known only to God.

THE MARTYR

The martyr slept under
The post office verandah,
One leg gone to the cause
Of the missionary church.
He owned one crutch and a blanket
And his hair spun from his head
Like bloodied hungry snakes.
His eyes of religion burned Kisii town.
In the morning cool
They gave the martyr
Food for the day
And he went to his secret place—
To pray?
Under the verandah of tin
He slept his nights
With a wild sentry dog.

AN AFRICAN I MET

He showed me his bag
Green like the hills
Ripening with coffee and tea,
Pyrethrum and passion fruit,
The bag over his left hand
That he showed
As he removed the sheath.
His long arching nails,
Fingernails curving
Discolored from light's lack,
Five nails twelve inches each
He held up like
The charmer's snake
Stiffened by the charmer's call.

ABUYA'S LAUGH

The village idiot
Wore clothes as though
Lion clawed
And ran to strangers
To throw words of shame
In their shaven faces.
He jumped in their path
And followed like a fly
Around an albino bull.
The vulgar left hand,
Palm up,
Abuya thrust in front
And in his hollow smile
Laughed for the ebony town.

ITINERANT WITCHDOCTOR

You brought your wares
For me to see:
Bottles filled blue,
Red,
Yellow the shade of gooseberries
And a mirror of magic.
But you wore no
Belt of cowrie shells,
No ostrich egg
Hung from your neck.
What use are the songs
You sing
When you speak no Gusii?
Your clothes have the cut
Of a Nairobi politician
And you use dark glasses
Like a man with no eyes.
They use your medicine:
The girls with short skirts,
Women who sell themselves
At the bus depot,
And salesmen whose
Spears refuse to lance.
But the children of Mogusii
Call Obara, the doctor,
Invite sorcerers by name,
Use diviners
Who know the power
Of the *omotembe* tree.

I SNAPPED HER PICTURE

She sells her goods
In the Thursday market,
The medicine of the old ones
She lays on her hide.
The bed maker who carries
His bed on his back
Stops to look at the
Shed snake skins,
Severed rats' tails,
And feathers of power birds.
She smiles at me,
The baby-colored man,
Taker of pills,
Mzungu with soles as soft
As the inside of thighs.

HE HELD MY HAND

He took my hand by
Manga Hill, Osoro did,
In Nyaribari where the great lake's
Finger at Homa Bay
Floats in a haze
Past banana plants and cotton flats.
My face blanched like
The palms of his black hands
Then scarlet like the coffee berries
When he held my hand,
A friendship sign to be
Shared in an afternoon of honey beer.
My mind raced frightened of beds
Yet he never heard of such things
Or dreamed of lover men.

A DISTRICT OFFICER

The man in charge of furniture
Can dull the fire of a flame tree
And roll his belly over his trouser top.
His hand is on the telephone
Waiting for important calls
And his voice sticks like unbaked dough.
He demands our tables,
Our bed and mattress,
The government chairs;
Then notes our name in a ledger
As though consigning us to hell.
But the days are warm,
The nights are cool,
And a floor is good
For an ailing back.

HUNGER

1.

Propped in
A shoebox crib,
He watched with lemon eyes.
He wore a spray of translucent hair
And his bareboned arms bore
Needle prints and the press of nurses' hands.
Illusions pumped his stomach full
And like paper exposed too long,
His skin faded yellow and brittle.

When I hold my children
And hear them laugh,
I occasionally wonder:

Did he live
To taste the sweet bananas,
Harvest gardens of millet and maize,
Tend the family herd on green hillsides,
Or did he die
Forever the infant of death?

2.

Bottles are bullets
Placed in infants' mouths,
Plastic missiles shot
For ivory and gold.
Peasant breasts drip their life
On children's graves
Inscribed with the word 'progress.'
Eyes in glass buildings
Never see the little mounds
But count them daily
In their profit reports.

EX-CHIEF MUSA

1.

Musa had no teeth
But held several gold medals
Awarded by the King.
The republican commissioner
Stripped him of his title,
But Musa kept his top hat
To salute America.
Twelve wives lived on one side
Of the fence
Another in his house,
Pleased in his conversion to
Pious Christianity.
He had seen giant babies with
Sticks of fire hold the hills
And disappear with the locust.
Musa, known as senior chief,
Fifty-six times a father.

2.

His son
Had wives of his own,
But Musa could never
Speak of such things
In front of him.
He sent Ogaro
From our home
To wait in the garden
Beside their British car.
Then he talked:
To Lyn not-yet-mother
Me with fresh-grown beard,
As though we lacked all gender
As though we had no age.
Old Musa spoke to us of sex.

GRANDMOTHER

"A story I am coming,"
And she talks of the beast Nyamongo
And the rooster-man Sakawa
Who melted at Nyanchwa hill.
The old woman draws on her pipe
While the young children listen.
She begins and
A story she becomes.

A LECTURE

As full as the
Fruit of a sausage tree,
Her breast she pulled
From the high-dress top
Waiting for her teetering son,
My Swahili speech stuttered.
She sat in the front
To see the thin teacher
From the far white land,
And she asked:
No children after a year?
How much did your bride-price cost?
Why one wife only,
You man of great wealth?

PRESIDENT MZEE KENYATTA

The President Visits

Abuya,
Dressed in his shredded best,
Directed phantom traffic
With an official wave.
One man blew a huge *rirandi* horn
Once used to call men to war.
Mzee Kenyatta
Flicked his whisk
Cut from a desert horse
And rode through town,
His eyes detention-camp worn.
From his dark heart-face,
Mzee wore a freedom smile.

Kenyatta in Kisii

With prison wire
Still in his eyes,
The President came
Flush with freedom.
He swished his whisk
As if clearing the sky
Of final nightmares.
His hat sparkled
Like colored shells
Washed on the equator shore.
Dancers chanted in circles,
Warriors held their shields.
Across the sky
White trails of vanishing silver birds.

BUS RIDE

The upcountry bus
Lurches with jokes,
They elude me.
People chew red stalks
Offer me some.
(Is it washed?)
I say no.
Dust sticks to my skin.

A stop:
Sunwarm coke,
Empty-frame glasses sell
For a shilling or less.
Chickens, sweat
Render open windows
Helpless.
Pissing men continue
Their talk beside the bus.
On the Nyanza plain
I see a cow
Hung from a tree.

REPATRIATED

(Perhaps as many as 100 youth, age 11-15, have been taken from Kisii by racketeers and forced to work as virtual slave labour in sawmills on farms in the Moshi area.

—Kenya Daily Nation, *March 19, 1966)*

Silently
They waited,
Standing like cords
Of dark wood
Cut in the forest of
Slave labour.
They stood in flatback trucks
In the government square,
The official plaza deserted,
The flagpole bare.
Then hill farmers came
To claim their children.
Unsmiling,
Without a word,
The families united
Walked home again
In the quiet
Of a Sunday afternoon.

INTERRUPTED HIKE

Wazungu don't walk
Or ride bicycles up hills.
They don't use country busses
Filled with chickens and goats.
Stop, *wazungu,*
Your feet will hurt.
Stop, *wazungu,*
Keep your feet soft,
Keep your feet clean.
We heard in America
You are born with wheels,
Your piss is gasoline.
Eeee, *wazungu.*
Wazungu, don't walk!

Wazungu—Swahili for Europeans or Americans.

GIFT GIVING

The plane put down.
Cows and cowherds
Greeted the Ambassador,
Not knowing what to say.
A politician from Wanjare location
Shook hands for American aid.
White cars waited,
Then like gifts of lightning,
Struck Suneka, Tabaka, and Kisii
With a promise of manna.
        Food for the hungry
        Work for the poor
        New skills for women's hands
"*Jambo*" and "*Kwa heri,*"
He said,
And returned to Nairobi
For golden reports via diplomatic pouch
And modest notes released to the press.
In western highland hills
        Yellow corn fit only for pigs
        A factory with nothing to make
        Weaving hands minus a loom

Jambo, kwa heri—Swahili for "hello," "good-bye."

FOR NKAKUNDI, OUR SON

1.

Beyond Kikuyu donkey carts,
Darting gazelles in the Great Rift,
We traveled withour new-born son—
Past the land of Maasai—
Drinkers of milk mixed with blood—
West of Kipsigis country where
Men stretch their earlobes long
And monkeys swing from forest trees:
We returned exultant.
Songs of praise
They sung,
Gifts they brought
(The women we knew)
To our cool wood house
And danced the afternoon
To our white infant son.

2.

Our eyes glitter
In the twilight sky.
Our children give us strength
And cause our eyes to shine.
Come, Moraa,
We'll churn milk and together
Sing of the mystery.
Your first-born cries—
Give him food,
Let him drink.
Now you know:
Beauty never ends,
Beauty never dies.
Dance with us,
Sing with us,
Sunset eyes.

TREPANNING

A razor blade
An old rusted chisel:
My God, she didn't cry!
Her husband held her pain
As the doctor peeled the scalp
Like a black cherry.
Her legs stick straight,
She sat and I looked
In dread amazement.
The master sculptor
Carved his work
To remove dung and worms and dirt
Poured from the sky.
Cow's fat washed her head
White with bone.
With her skull scraped clean,
Her husband dried her sweat with leaves.
Then slowly she walked home to sleep.

NUBIAN WEDDING

With blazing heads
Of vermilion scarves,
Women beat a circle dance
Near the raw white mosque.
For the wedding they came
And spread their gifts on
Raffia rugs.
Ululations like excited birds
Flew through the air
While I sat in the groom's dark hut
With red-eyed men
And watched them quietly drink
Away their fear.

CELEBRATION

Circumcision Song

Obara is crying,
Whose child is this?
Prepare a shield,
Forge a spear,
Now he can do anything,
Onsario, your son.
You are no longer a boy,
You who have felt pain.
Obara, the doctor,
Cries with your pain
And uses your foreskin
To store millet.
Spear your mother.
Otete nyoko!
Come along shining—
Blind the Maasai.
Otete nyoko, Eeee!
You are a man today.

Nyansarara's Circumcision

With skirts bunched manshaped,
Women sing down the macadam road.
Ululations call birds
To see them dance around
Nyansarara eleven with blood
Awake before the sun.
With sticks whipping the air,
Men-women sing the songs of sex.
She stands blood wet
Between her legs of strength.
Her mock maleness gone,
Nyansarara has a woman become.

Otete nyoko—Gusii (language of the Kisii) choral chant during male puberty rite signifying that the male is sexually mature.

SONG OF PRAISE

We shine like the nylon
That hangs in Kisii shops,
Our skin clean and handsome.
Listen to the *obokano* playing
Like a giant songbird.
Come join our dance slowly.
Friends eat our white ants
And share our ground nuts.
Our hills turn red with coffee cherries,
Turn yellow with sweet bananas.
By our strong hands
We have brought great wealth
From the red earth of Wanjare.
We sing with the morning rise.

Obokano—Gusii for a huge lyre-like instrument.

BEER PARTY SONG

Look at Mokera:
He cries because his
Cows are gone.
They disappeared in the night,
Stolen while he snored.
He is too poor to marry now
And Kemunto dances with someone else.
There she goes, Mokera.
She talks to another about marriage.
Listen to Mokera:
He asks his father for money
But gets enough only for cigarettes.
Mokera, there are cows in the valley
By the Kuja River,
The mottled bull looks like yours.
Ask the thief to give them back,
Tell him you are crying for Kemunto.
How beautiful she is
Dancing there by the beer pot.
Mokera, you are a fool.
Woman, dance!

SELF-PITY

Neighbors laugh.
They say you eat eggs
When I'm not at home
And hide chickens for yourself.

You let goats and dogs in the house,
They trample the pots to broken heaps.
You act like a hopping crow that
Lays its eggs then cares nothing
For its nest.

Why do you compare me to
Sagini and Nyamwea?
They take my tax money
Then ride to meetings in swollen cars.

Once I had cows enough to marry
And you rubbed yourself with ghee.
Now thieves have taken all the cows
And your skin cuts like porcupine quills.

You quarrel in front of guests,
Calling evil to our home.
Shameless woman,
Pour me more millet beer.

A FUNERAL

"From the leopard clan
Someone came
And bewitched my brother.
Beware,
You who have abused
My mother.
Take notice of her womb.
Manyara, do you see my tears?
Brother, they are for you.
We are taken by death
One by one."

Without her clothes
The woman ran
By the banana tree grave.
The mourners stood
Silent.
One drum played
Above her screams
And a young man sang.

LOCUST SONG

They come flying
From Manga's far side,
The sky storm-grey
With thunderous wings.
Chinsaga they eat,
Strip our white maize bare,
Consume all the millet.
They make the garden bitter
Like death.
Mothers will boil tobacco,
Make tea without milk.
Our shields will not protect,
Our spears fall empty.
God, keep us alive.
Keep us alive, O God!

Chinsaga—Gusii for a vegetable similar to collard greens.

MAASAI MARKET

1.

Young boys walk about
Selling buckets of blood—
Blood to drink
Mixed with urine and milk.
And flies are drawn
To ochre-dyed hair
To rest around eyes
That watch our moves
Unblinking.

2.

One day
In a little cafe
On a muddy street
You ran your finger on my lip
And touched the soft hair on my arm.
I looked at your orange ochre hair
Braided as warriors do
And admired the bracelets on your wrist,
Around your young dark leg.
Then our shadows disengaged.
Mine forever a darker shade of black.

CATTLE TENDING

A Flute Player

Cow bells ring
To the slow sound
Of shuffled hooves.
        a flute
        by the acacia grove
On the
Brown savannah
A musician plays
His solitaire song.

At the Migori River

Do they sing of us
On the Mara plain,
The two Maasai who
Stood like black flamingo?
Are there songs of us
On the open land
About pallor and shoes,
Hair as thick as rock
Baboons?
I still hear
Bells of a thousand cows unseen
And see two warriors watching,
Ready.

YOUNG WOMEN

Rachel

Liquid
Like silk,
Rachel:
Black gazelle . . .
No, leopard.

Turkana Girl

On the morning sand
A body arabesque
Catches the sun
In two shades of black.
She plaits her hair,
Winds wire jewels
Against her throat:
A desert girl sits
Like a sacred speckled bird
Of the ancient river Nile.

SUICIDE

He died on the lakeshore—
John Parrot—
The white who cut
Ocean waves with his body
And broke color bars
With his walk
On St. Augustine's beach.

"Find Parrot!"

We searched the country
Of Maasai near Kilgoris,
Looked in Kuria homes
Around Masara.
We sent word out.
And he lay still
As jackals hid him in caves
And vultures carried him
To the sun.

WITCHING

1.

An exorcist:
Sniffing the trail of evil.

2.

Priapism,
The devil's mark,
Given the magic hand
For manhood's knife.

3.

Nightwatch
At fresh gravesides.
Witching ghouls
Run naked.

TO THE EDGE OF THE EARTH

Two Giraffes

Golden,
Mist-eaters on
Sunrise hills
Lope beside our train,
Gentle.

Mistaken Identity

Randy from the sun,
The elephant bull—
Five-legged strong.
Our car, a cow
Demurely squat
On grazing-land grass.

On the Narok Road

By the green thorn tree
Gentle giants like
Tawny papyrus reeds.
Zebra, gazelle graze.
In the shadow
Of the volcano glen—
A lion?
Wildebeest,
Crazed creatures,
Kick, butt—stop and start.
In dust clouds
Ostrich gallop off
To the edge of the earth.

THE GREAT MIGRATION

They don't know bridges
Or murram tourist roads.
They follow the smell of rain
And in a tribe of a million hooves
Cross transparent boundaries.
No one will miss a dozen
Dragged into the storming river,
Stinking on the rocks.
Vultures, sitting in cozy pairs,
Savor the stench of their feast.
Hippos sleep indolently
And buffaloes raise their lazy heads.
There's no need of tombstones here.

BIRDS

1.

Golden crowns of feathers
Flash.
Two crested cranes
Fitfully strut their mating dance
Outside the meeting hall window.

2.

In towering eucalyptus
Unseen lovers call
As if one-bird voice.

3.

Hung from a gum tree,
Weavers build their
City of nests,
As raucous as the Thursday market.

4.

Sunbird,
Little nectar thief
Shimmering green, blue
Across the garden,
Enjoy my lemon flowers.

5.

The pink beach of Nakuru
Scatters skyward at
Our advance—
A million flamingoes.

6.

In front of our Rover
The grey man flew
From the red dust road.
Ah, a giant stork.

LONELY FASCINATION

The crane with the broken wing
Is not the ancient boy caressing
His own reflection.
By the long window panes
He preens and dances
As a hopeful mate,
Condemned forever to hours
Of lonely fascination,
Charming his solitary heart.

CREATURES

1.

Across Malindi mud
Comrade ants,
Combat strong,
Troop to their cause.

2.

My wall,
Heavy with snores.
A bee's nest hidden.

3.

Unfelt,
I'm pricked.
Bedbugs leave me
Measle-marked for days.

4.

Wood-fat borers.
Turn by turn
Sawdust beams on
Our garden porch.

5.

Roach,
Stop!
I have greetings
From your Hackensack cousins.

SHAPES

The womb swells round
With fertilized seed.
Mud houses share the
Shape of the earth.
The hot circle, the white disc
Bring warmth and fecundity.
A child must drink from
Breasts full and heavy.
But the snake has its place
And must be worshipped too.

A CHORUS MOVING

A dozen crested cranes.
No one looked up but me.
I wandered the market beyond the hill
Alone in my color and thoughts.
The center flew apart
Like a startled flock.
Someone lacked a ticket to sell,
The guard chased her from her place.
Then they settled again
As if returning to roost.
The girls are like that, too,
Gathering slowly in the darkening sky,
A few voices soft in song.
Like a breeze gathering strength
Their voices take shape
And one tune fills the dark.
I see a chorus moving
But my ears are stuffed with western ways.

NAIROBI TAN

There is a
Smell of ginger about.
And shops overflow
With silks and spices.
At the right time of year
Jivanjee Garden becomes
Lavender soft with
Fallen petals from
Jacaranda trees.
The temple stands
Permanently girdled
By lights strung like
Colored stars.
In brown cafes
The languages of India
Swirl in air deep
With pastime sweets.
By pastel suburbs
There is the swish of saris.
All feet are sandaled.

Nairobi tan
On the way
To upland black.

THE COAST

Dhows once carried
Human cargo through these ports
And chests of stolen ivory and clove
Smashed against the avenging coral reef.
Now tourists come to play
In the Indian sea and darken on the sand.
Mangroves tangle as if in endless struggle
And palm trees tower like guards
Against slave ships.
Behind hotels and swimming pools,
A deserted city lies in stone heaps.
They come to play on sand
As white as bleached bone
And, like the ghosts of slave-traders,
Linger with the shark.

LAKE RUDOLF

The moon shines cold
On the desert
And the endless wind
Moves low through the grass,
Spraying sand against my tent.
Crocodile eyes,
Like drops of blood,
Spread across the lake water.
One sheet is too thick
As my body burns
Worlds away from home.

UGANDA

Twilight

Seven hills rise
In Kampala,
Each crowned with
A temple raised
To a separate god.
And fruit-tree bats
With pulsing flight
Darken the Nile-dusk sky.

Two Nights in Uganda

Behind the temple gates
Purple and white
Came prayers and drums
From the sacred book of Granth
And Sikh voices before the
Songs of morning birds.
We journeyed to Fort Portal
At the bottom of the Mountains
Of the Moon
And slept in a house
Owned by a Toro princess—
An empty house,
Her highness officially deposed.
Through the night we listened
To bat wings flap
In vacant rooms.

CANES

I saw a man caned.
His back liquid red and black
Defied the flying strokes.
His face was turned from mine.
A mother drew a switch over her shoulder.
The child too young for trousers
Wept up the hill.
Students suffer teachers' blows.
But Nyalinda told me she trembled
At the voice of an American nun.
"Under her apron. Was that a
Heavy grey gun?"
And, at the Kisii hotel,
Kimante afraid of shoot-outs
On my cities' streets.
Wheat blows golden over silent holes.
Planes hiss unseen over the Rockies,
One hundred thousand have cold mouths of dirt.
The world waits the final lash,
And I watch one cane scald an iron back.

THE MISSION

1.

The fence is in,
The leaves are dying brown.
Barbed wire has been ordered
And will be set as the fresh wood dries.
It is a Catholic fence
Marking off the compound.
Prayers echo in the rock church,
Thorns of red flowers grow by the door.
Still silver the leaves,
Tomorrow to be filled with poison teeth.

2.

Unrelieved lamentation,
Hands frozen in pity,
You're ringed by foreign flowers,
Strangers in Papal dress.
A stone shawl hangs on your shoulders.
Alexander, your creator, is now one-eyed
And half-dead on millet beer.
White madonna with African lips;
You watch the west
And wait for black angels.

CRUEL EYES

The childless father
Gives sweets to his children.
His pockets sag like his paunch
And they all know the smell
Of colored sugar.
He gives, tosses the drops
To the trailing swarm,
And smiles.

And I remember:
Early evening,
A Long Island beach.
We threw scraps
Into the summer sky.
Gulls churned the air
With darting wings,
Grabbing pieces to our applause.

At half a chance
They would eat our cruel eyes.

THE BUTCHER SHOP

The blade and rock scrape in conspiracy.
We won't go back
But sit on a wooden bench.
A muddy ewe trails her tether,
Bleats in the butcher's hands.
We talk about the roads to Kisii.
Dogs with ribs rubbing against their fur
Bark behind the shop.
We see no blood running
But the air leaves no doubt.
The dogs lick the chopping block.
The warm meat is heavy in my hand,
It is steaming in my Judas hand.

FREEDOM

Where is the man
Who turns Africa free?
Nyangati marries another
For the first bears only girls.
Ongesa refuses his the post-box key,
It's too precious for a woman to hold.
Not one woman carves the quarried stone,
Not one forms her lips to whistle.
Where is the woman
To set Africa free?

OLD PEOPLE

The old man carves
    The old man sits on a bench
The old man watches his cows
    The old man watches strangers pass by
The old man greets his grandchildren
    The old man reads last year's letter
The old woman grinds her maize
    The old woman turns her thumbs
The old woman tells night-time stories
    The old woman talks to herself
There is light in the home. Children laugh.
    There is the shuffle of slippered feet.

KISII WARRIORS

With shields of hippo hides
And spears sharp,
They were warriors.
Horns sang of war,
Voices sang with victory.
They feared no Maasai,
No Luo, no Kipsigis.
They killed a white officer near Getembe,
No settler could take their land,
The warriors of Kisii.
Now the songs lament,
Sigh about defeated love and thieves
Who steal an old woman's slip.
O warriors!
The warriors.
They drink millet beer
With the first light of day
And fall on their faces under the moon.
The warriors are brave
Around an earthen beer pot.
They fight with slurred words
And think their straws are spears,
The warriors of Kisii.
The storms that blow from Manga hill,
The rains that drown the crops,
It is Mogusii who cries
Remembering the true warriors
The men who could walk upright.

FOR OUR AMERICAN-BORN GIRL

Osoro, my name,
Moraa, your mother.
And brother Nyankundi
Circled with newborn songs.
Your name comes on wings
From the white hill Tabaka.
Kwamboka
They give you,
The child from the
River's far side.
Now you too can shine
With the Kisii sun.

SIMPLE THINGS

Nothing is shrill.
The nearest telephone
Rings two valleys away.
The golden dog cools in the shade.
We listen to our latest letter,
Bathe in a metal bowl,
Savor one chocolate bar.
My tea is amber,
Come sit with me in the dim light.
Look—
Our children smile in their sleep.

GOING HOME

I want to show you my city, too:
Slowly bleeding,
Stabbing the sky with glassy knives
And sheltering ragged armies
In glassy shadows.
You can burn your eyes out,
Charcoal your lungs,
Turn your soul to stone.
Men smear asphalt across meadows
Where I come from.
I'll show you America's jewel.
I'm going home in time
For the autumn show.

POSTCRIPT

All that is haze now
And beyond my touch
Like the clouds below:
    rocky walks
    harvest maize
    smiles with milky tea
    and a cobra
Your three-stone fire burns
And from the rafters calabash gourds.
You are velvet as strong as steel
Sewn in my dreamy words.

One thousand copies of
SUNBIRD
were printed for this
first edition.
The first two hundred
have been signed
by the author
and the artist
of which
this book is

____